D0454872

The Catholic Children's Prayer Book

The Catholic Children's Prayer Book

By
LOUIS M. SAVARY

Illustrations by
RITA GOODWILL

Cover illustration by
GEORGE ANGELINI

REGINA PRESS
New York

Imprimatur:
C. Eykens, Vic. gen.
Antverpiae, 6 junii 1985

1985
THE REGINA PRESS
7 Midland Avenue
Hicksville, N.Y. 11802

Book design and typography by Roth Advertising

ISBN: 0-88271-127-X

Printed in Belgium

*Gratefully dedicated
to the memory of
Frank San Chirico,
a devoted and loyal friend
of The Regina Press
for over fifty years.*

A PREFACE

Addressed to Parents and Teachers

This is an effort to write a contemporary prayer book for children.

The first objective was to make the book *complete*. To do this, much historical and catechetical information has been supplied. The book is both a prayer book and a catechism. It also includes guides for Christian living.

A second objective was to construct a prayer book that was immersed in the Catholic *tradition*. So prayers like the Way of the Cross, the Rosary, Litanies, and devotions to the Saints have been included. It also contains traditional catechetical materials such as the Ten Commandments, Precepts of the Church, the Beatitudes, The Corporal and Spiritual Works of Mercy, and brief explanations of the Seven Sacraments.

A third objective was to make the book *contemporary,* so that its underlying theology of prayer and the church would be in line with what is currently taught in seminaries. The eucharistic liturgy is presented in accordance with the renewal developing since Vatican II; the approach to the Sacraments, especially Reconciliation, reflects the Church's current teaching.

If you are enthusiastic about prayer and hope this book can help your child, let your enthusiasm and love show.

The best way for a child to learn to pray is *to pray with you.*

LOUIS M. SAVARY, S.T.D.
*Completed on March 30, 1985
the birthday of my mother,
who taught me to pray as a child.*

TABLE OF CONTENTS

Chapter 1

WHO IS GOD?

The most important question in anyone's life is *Who is God?*

Your answer to it makes all the difference in the world.

God is the most important being there is.

God made everything—the earth, the sun, the stars, the animals, and human beings.

God created the entire universe, from the smallest insect to the tallest tree, from a drop of rain to the mighty oceans.

God made you. He made your body. He made your soul that gives life to your body, that talks with your lips, that looks through your eyes.

God is good. God is holy.

God lives always. God was before the beginning of the universe. God will be even when the universe ends.

God is everywhere. God is in heaven and on earth. God is in the air, beneath the sea and in the center of a mountain. God is present at your side and also on the farthest star.

God knows all things. God sees you, hears you, knows what you think and say and do. God watches over you lovingly.

God loves all things. God loves you with an infinite love. God loves you more than your mother or father ever could.

God made you to know Him, to serve Him and to love Him, so that you may be happy with Him now and in the life to come.

Jesus told us that God's name is love.

There is only one God.

Yet God is a Trinity. That means in God's nature there are three Persons.

God's three Persons are named Father, Son and Holy Spirit.

GOD THE FATHER

God the Father is the creator of the world. He has wonderful plans for all of us who live in the world.

In His love, we are meant to become one big loving community in which everyone knows and cares about each other. That is the Father's grand plan.

Jesus was the one who told us that God's name is Father. Actually Jesus' word for Him was "Abba," which means "Dad" or "Daddy." God is a Father who loves us very much.

Sad to say, human beings turned away from God again and again. They turned away by committing serious sin.

Sin created big problems in God's plan. People rejected God and His love and began creating their own plans.

In order to tell people they were forgiven and to remind them of God's plan for unity, God sent His only Son to earth to accomplish this mission.

GOD THE SON

God's Son became human and took to himself a body and a soul like yours. That is what we mean by the *Incarnation*.

God's Son received the name Jesus and was born of the Virgin Mary. He lived on our planet for thirty-three years. He offered himself as a sacrifice to the Father. His sacrifice was to suffer and die on the cross for the forgiveness of all human sins. This is what we mean by Redemption.

During his life on earth, Jesus reminded us of God's plan to make us all into one loving community. This community would be called the Body of Christ.

And so Jesus overcame sin and was soon to return to his Abba. But he promised to send us the Holy Spirit to carry on the great work of unity.

The Holy Spirit is the third Person of the divine Trinity.

GOD THE HOLY SPIRIT

The Holy Spirit is the Father's Spirit. The Holy Spirit is also Jesus' Spirit. The Holy Spirit is the real presence of God in our heart and soul.

We are living in the Age of the Holy Spirit.

The Holy Spirit came first to Jesus' disciples on the day we celebrate as Pentecost.

Afterward, the Holy Spirit came to all those who believed in Jesus.

The Holy Spirit brings gifts to each of us if we are open to them. Jesus said we would be able to do great things with the power of the Holy Spirit.

The Holy Spirit has one great task: to build the Mystical Body of Christ into a loving unity.

When the Holy Spirit's task is done, we will all be together, loving and caring for each other. And that will be Heaven.

Here on earth, one of the most powerful ways of helping to build the Body of Christ is prayer.

All of this book is about prayer.

PRAYERS TO THE TRINITY

The Sign of the Cross

Whenever you make the Sign of the Cross, you bless your body, mind and spirit in the name of the Blessed Trinity.

Here is how to do it.

With the tip of your right hand, touch your forehead and say, *"In the name of the Father. "*

Next, touch your chest and say, *"and of the Son."*

Then touch your left and right shoulders and say, *"and of the Holy Spirit. Amen."*

In this way you mark your body with God's names. God will protect you and keep you from harm. It reminds you of the cross on which Jesus died for love of you.

Glory Be

Another very familiar prayer of praise to the Blessed Trinity is the following:

*Glory be to the Father
and to the Son
and to the Holy Spirit,
as it was in the beginning,
is now and ever shall be,
world without end. Amen.*

Chapter 2

WHAT IS PRAYER?

Prayer is making special time for God.

Prayer is something everyone can do. Whether you are healthy or sick, happy or sad, rich or poor, you can always pray.

Children's prayers are among the most powerful. Jesus could never resist a child's prayer.

Remember that. You can have great power in heaven if you are a child who prays.

WAYS OF PRAYER

There are many ways of praying.

You will learn some of them in this book.

Some prayers are made up of certain words, as the *Our Father* and the *Hail Mary*. They are recited in the same way whenever we say them.

Sometimes you can make up the words of a prayer yourself. For example, you may ask God in your own words to bless your mother and father.

Other prayers use only thoughts and desires. No words are spoken. Such prayer is called *meditation*. In meditation we think about God and desire to be with Him.

Other prayer happens in our imagination. The *Rosary* and the *Way of the Cross* are like this. Using your imagination in prayer is sometimes called *contemplation*.

Some prayers involve our bodies. When you make *The Sign of the Cross*, you use your hands and arms. Some people pray to God with their bodies by dancing and singing.

So you see there are many ways of praying.

THE IMPORTANT THING

The important thing in every way of praying is getting in touch with God, or the angels and saints.

Prayer means bringing your attention to God, and spending time with God.

It means lifting your mind and heart and body to God and to the things of God.

So whether you use words, thoughts, or desires, whether you use your body or imagination, you will be praying when you communicate with God.

HOW TO PRAY

If you are as attentive to God as you are to your friends when they come to visit you and play with you, then your prayer will be beautiful.

God loves you more than any friend.

Since prayer is so special—having a visit and a conversation with God—pray with all your heart and with full attention.

Mean every word you say.

If you read prayers from a prayer book like this, read the words slowly and try to say them from your heart.

WHY DO WE PRAY?

We pray because we love God and want to be with God. We pray to show our *love* for God.

We pray to tell God we *join* Him in working together to bring all people to Jesus.

We pray to *praise* God, because of how wonderful God is, in his creation, in his forgiveness, in his justice, in his love.

We pray to *thank* God for all his gifts to us. Every good thing that happens to us comes from God.

We pray to say we are *sorry* to God for all the times we have not used his gifts or responded to his invitation to be kind and loving to others.

We pray to *ask* God for favors. We ask for the things we need or for what other people need. This is called a prayer of *petition*.

We also pray to the angels and saints asking them for favors and for help. The angels and saints are very close to God.

WHO PRAYS FOR ME?

Since we all belong to Christ, we all pray in the Holy Spirit.

This means we all live in the Holy Spirit as surely as we all live in the air we breathe.

In the Holy Spirit we are all related. And each person helps every other person in need, just as your right arm helps your left arm.

Pray for all those in your community who need help. Remember especially those who are closest to you: your parents, brothers and sisters, relatives and friends, priests, sisters and teachers.

They are the ones who pray for you, too. Just as you ask God to bless them, they ask God to bless you.

Whenever we pray, the Holy Spirit is in our heart praying with us.

Whenever we pray, all who believe in Jesus are with us.

We are never alone when we pray.

No one is ever forgotten by the Holy Spirit.

WHEN TO PRAY

Praying is like eating and breathing, we need to do it every day.

It helps if you have special times each day for praying. Ask your parents to help you always to remember:

Morning Prayer
Evening Prayers
Grace Before Meals
Grace After Meals
Mass on Sundays and Holy Days

Prayers for these times are in this prayer book.

Many Catholics also have special devotions to Mary, Joseph, and the other Saints. They like to say the *Rosary*, make the *Way of the Cross*, or recite *Litanies*.

Prayers for all of these times are also in this prayer book. We begin with the prayers that every child will want to learn by heart.

Chapter 3

IMPORTANT PRAYERS
TO BE LEARNED BY HEART

Certain prayers are so important and used so often that you will want to be able to say them without having to look in a prayer book.

You may know some of them already. If not, you can begin learning. One way to memorize prayers is to say them often.

As you learn a prayer, you should think about the words. Try to mean each word you say. After you learn prayers by heart, always say them *from* your heart.

A most important prayer to say from memory is the prayer Jesus taught his disciples to say. It is called *The Lord's*

Prayer or the *Our Father*. The gospel according to Matthew gives us the prayer in Jesus' own words.

The Lord's Prayer
(From Matthew 6:9–13)

Our Father, who art in heaven,
hallowed be Thy name,
Thy kingdom come,
Thy will be done,
on earth as it is in heaven.
Give us this day our daily bread,
and forgive us our trespasses
as we forgive those
who trespass against us,
and lead us not into temptation,
but deliver us from evil. Amen.

One of the favorite prayers of Catholics is the *Hail Mary*. Some of the prayer is taken from the angel's words that told Mary she would be Jesus' mother. Other

words are taken from the greeting Mary
received from her cousin Elizabeth.

The Hail Mary
(From Luke 1:28, 42)

Hail Mary, full of grace,
the Lord is with thee;
blessed art thou among women,
and blessed is the fruit
of thy womb, Jesus.
Holy Mary, Mother of God,
pray for us sinners now
and at the hour of our death. Amen.

The Apostles' Creed is a very ancient
prayer created by church leaders,
called Apostles, when the Christian
church was just beginning. It tells what
Christians believe about God the
Father, Jesus the Son, and the Holy
Spirit.

The Apostles' Creed

I believe in God,
the Father almighty
creator of heaven and earth.
I believe in Jesus Christ, his only Son,
our Lord. He was conceived
by the power of the Holy Spirit
and born of the Virgin Mary.
He suffered under Pontius Pilate,
was crucified, died, and was buried.
He descended to the dead.
On the third day he rose again.
He ascended into heaven,
and is seated at the right hand
of the Father.
He will come again
to judge the living and the dead.
I believe in the Holy Spirit,
the holy catholic Church,
the communion of saints,
the forgiveness of sins,
the resurrection of the body,
and the life everlasting. Amen.

Here are a few other prayers you will want to learn by heart.

Glory Be to the Father

Glory be to the Father
and to the Son,
and to the Holy Spirit.
As it was in the beginning,
is now, and ever shall be,
world without end. Amen.

Act of Faith

O my God, I believe that you are
one God in three Divine Persons:
Father, Son and Holy Spirit.
I believe that Your Divine Son
became Man and died for our sins,
and that He will come again to
judge the living and the dead.
I believe these and all the truths
that the Catholic Church teaches,
because You have revealed them,
who can neither deceive nor
be deceived. Amen.

Act of Hope

O my God, relying on Your
almighty power and infinite mercy
and promises, I hope to obtain
pardon of my sins, the help
of Your grace and life everlasting
through the merits of Jesus Christ,
my Lord and Redeemer. Amen.

Act of Love

O my God, I love You above all things
with my whole heart and soul,
because You are all good
and worthy of all love.
I love my neighbor as myself
for the love of You.
I forgive all who have injured me
and ask pardon of all
whom I have injured. Amen

Prayer to the Holy Spirit

Come, O Holy Spirit, fill the hearts
of your faithful and kindle in them
the fire of Your love.

> V. Send forth Your Spirit
>   and they shall be created.

> R. And You shall renew the face
>   of the earth.

Let us pray:
O God, who has taught the hearts
of the faithful by the light
of the Holy Spirit,
grant that in the same Spirit,
we may be always truly wise
and ever rejoice
in His consolation.
Through Christ our Lord. Amen.

Chapter 4

MORNING PRAYERS

The best way for a Christian child to begin each day is with morning prayers.

As soon as you wake up, let your first thoughts go to God.

Thank God for keeping you safe all night and for giving you a brand new day in which to enjoy life. Reverently mark your body with the *Sign of the Cross.*

Many children kneel down at their bedside as soon as they rise. It is not necessary to kneel while saying your morning prayers. But kneeling can be a sign of your special love and reverence for God.

Sometimes when you awake, you may be in a hurry to go somewhere or do something. That is why it is helpful to learn your morning prayers by heart.

When you learn prayers by heart, you can close your eyes when you say them, and really concentrate.

Or else you can keep your prayer book by your bed, and put a marker in the place where your morning prayers begin.

You don't have to say many prayers in the morning. The important thing is that you tell God that you love him.

Here are some prayers from which you can choose.

FAMILIAR PRAYERS

In Chapter 3, you learned to say *The Lord's Prayer, The Hail Mary, the Glory be,* and *the Apostles' Creed.* These are fine morning prayers.

Short Morning Prayers

Each of these prayers takes only a few moments to say.

God, I believe all the truths which you have taught us.

God, I hope for your grace on earth and for eternal life with you in heaven.

God, I love you with all my heart and soul.

God, I am sorry for all my sins. Help me never to commit them any more.

O sweetest Heart of Jesus,
I implore that I may ever love you
more and more.

Mary, you are my loving mother.
Keep me near you and your dear son,
Jesus, today.

Saint Joseph, watch over me today
just as you protected and cared
for the Child Jesus.

Angel of God, my guardian dear,
To whom His love commits me here,
Ever this day be at my side
To light and guard, to rule and guide.
Amen.

Morning Offering

Many Catholics each morning offer all they do to be joined together with all the prayers and masses throughout the world. They dedicate their thoughts and acts to the Hearts of Jesus and Mary.

First is a very simple version of the Morning Offering, followed by the one many adults say.

O Sacred Heart of Jesus,
I offer you this day
all my thoughts, words,
desires, and actions. Help me do
everything for you.

O, Jesus, through the Immaculate
Heart of Mary, I offer You
my prayers, works, joys
and sufferings of this day
in union with the holy Sacrifice
of the Mass throughout the world.
I offer them for all the intentions
of Your Sacred Heart:
the salvation of souls,
reparation for sin,
the reunion of all Christians;
I offer them for the intentions
of our bishops and
of all members
of the Apostleship of Prayer,
and in particular
for those recommended
by our Holy Father this month.

Chapter 5

EVENING PRAYERS

Just as you say "Good night" to your mother and father each evening, so you say "Good night" to God.

Kneel by your bed, make the Sign of the Cross, and spend a few minutes with God.

Thank God for having kept you safe during the day. Ask God to forgive you the unkind things you may have done. Promise to do better tomorrow.

Tell God again and again that you love Him.

If you need help in your prayers, here are some suggestions.

Say the **Our Father,** the **Hail Mary,** and the **Glory Be.**

I adore You, God, I belong entirely
to you. I kneel in your presence and
and adore You, my Lord and my God.

I thank you, God, for keeping me
safe all day. Watch over me tonight.
All that I have and all that I am,
I have received from you.

I believe that you are here, God.
I lay myself down to rest in Your sight.

I hope, God, that you will protect
me always, day and night, and will
bring me safely through the years
of this life to the dawn of eternity.

I love you, God. You are all good
and I shall never stop loving You.
Teach me to love you more each day.

Mother Mary, pray for me to Jesus
who so often went to sleep
in your arms.

Saint Joseph, who watched over
the Child Jesus,
keep watch over me this night.

My Guardian Angel, remain by my side
every hour of the day and night.

Jesus, bless my father and mother,
and all those whom I love.
(You may give the names of others
you wish God specially to bless.)

Jesus, have mercy on the poor souls
in purgatory. Help them come to You.

DURING-THE-DAY PRAYERS

A very natural time to say thanks to God is just before you begin eating each meal. And afterwards, too.

GRACE BEFORE MEALS

Bless us, O Lord,
and these Your gifts
which we are about to receive
from Your bounty
through Christ our Lord. Amen.

GRACE AFTER MEALS

We give You thanks,
O almighty God,
for all Your benefits;
You who live and reign,
world without end. Amen.

Chapter 6

HOLY MASS
The Eucharistic Celebration

The most important prayer for Catholics is the Mass. This Eucharistic celebration is the public celebration of our union with Christ and our life in the Body of Christ.

The congregation gathers together at the church. In joy and thanksgiving, they announce God's love and forgiveness to the world.

At Mass we sing songs of praise that affirm our belief in Jesus. We recite prayers of petition confidently, knowing in faith that our Redeemer lives in our hearts and loves us.

It is very important for you to attend Mass every Sunday and Holy Day. At Mass is where you most fully express your faith in a public way.

The world needs to know how important it is to worship God. Going to Mass is your way of telling the world how important God is in your life.

At Mass is where you meet the others in your community who believe in Jesus. At church is where you greet them, encourage them, and wish them the Peace of Christ.

At Mass is where you join your heart and voice in prayer with those who love God.

Among the people at Mass, you may find your best friends and those who have special concern for you. At Mass, you are safe and secure and well-loved.

LITURGY OF THE WORD

The first half of the Mass is called the Liturgy of the Word. (Liturgy means prayer done by a group of people.)

During this part of Mass, God comes to us, first, through the written word in the readings from the Bible. Second, God comes to us through the spoken word of the priest or deacon who gives the sermon or homily. (A homily explains the readings from the bible.)

It is important to listen to the readings and even to read them, if you can, silently along with the lector.

There is much to learn about God and the church from the readings and homily. The Gospel reading almost always contains the very words that Jesus spoke. How precious those words are to us!

LITURGY OF THE EUCHARIST

In this part of the Mass, God comes to us through the Eucharist, in Holy Communion.

We begin this part by offering gifts of bread and wine to God. These gifts symbolize the offering of ourselves to God.

When the priest consecrates the bread and wine, he repeats what Jesus did with bread and wine at the Last Supper.

As the priest says the words, "This is my body" over the bread, Christ comes and puts his very being into the bread. This same miracle happens when the priest says "This is the cup of my blood" over the wine.

We believe that Christ is really present in the bread and wine now, even though the bread still seems just bread and the wine seems just wine.

At the end of the Eucharistic Prayer,

the priest lifts up the consecrated bread
and wine as a sacrifice to God. Sacrifice
means to make something sacred or holy.
The Body and Blood of Christ is offered
to God as a sacrifice for our salvation.

Now we are ready for Holy Communion.

HOLY COMMUNION

During this final part of Mass, we
become especially conscious of our unity
as a community. It is a special time of
love and joy.

We greet all the people around us
with a handshake, or a hug, or a kiss,
and wish them, "The Peace of Christ".

We also remember the needs of other
human beings who are not present
with us at this time.

Now we are at peace and feel specially
close to God and his people all over the

world. We are ready to receive Holy Communion. How joyful a moment it is.

Jesus really and truly comes into our hearts in Holy Communion!

The Jesus we receive is the same Jesus who lived and died 2,000 years ago, and who arose from the dead and who is alive now and forever.

It is hard to explain a mystery of faith, but all who believe in Jesus are members of his Mystical Body. This means that all followers of Jesus on earth and in heaven are part of him.

Chapter 7

HOLY COMMUNION

Every time you receive Holy Communion, you are receiving a sacrament. So it is a special moment in your life, a moment of joy and love and blessing.

Like all special moments, you will want to prepare for it. Receiving Jesus in your body is like meeting an important guest. You will want to prepare your mind and heart before communion. You will also want to be clean and well-dressed to welcome your divine guest.

Let yourself be happy as you wait your turn to go up to the altar to receive. Tell Jesus that your heart is eager to have him come to visit you.

Suppose the Blessed Virgin were

placing the baby Jesus in your arms to hold for a little while? How eager you would be! How carefully you would hold him! How lovingly you would talk to him!

In communion, Jesus does even more. He enters your heart and soul and lives there.

Some of the following prayers will help you get ready for the moment of communion.

PRAYERS BEFORE COMMUNION

Jesus, soon I will be receiving you.
I cannot wait!
I want you very much to come to me!
Jesus, even though I do not deserve
to have you live in me,
I know you want to come.
Please make me ready to welcome you
into my heart.

Jesus, I am sorry for anything
I did to hurt you or other people.
I promise that I will try to be kind
and loving. I love you.

Jesus, I know you are God.
I thank you for coming to visit me.
Please stay with me always.
Be a friend in my heart.

Jesus, I give you my heart.
I love you very much.
This is all I have to offer you.

Jesus, I believe that I will
receive You in Holy Communion.
It is really you who will come
into my heart and soul. I must get ready
now.

Jesus, I want to open my heart
and soul to receive you.
I want you to fill me with your life.
I want to live with you forever.

PRAYERS AFTER COMMUNION

Jesus, you are in my soul
at this very moment. I love you.
I want you to stay with me.

Jesus, thank you. Thank you
for coming to me today.
You are a precious gift to me.

Jesus, now that you are within me,
I want to ask you to bless my family
and my friends, but especially
those who have no one
to pray for them.

Jesus, I believe in you,
I hope in you, I love you
above all things.

Jesus, see how little I am
and how much I need to grow.
Make my soul beautiful
so that you will stay
with me always.

Jesus, I offer you my body and soul,
my mind and all my energy.
Take me to yourself and let me feel
your love.

Jesus, bless my hands, my feet,
my eyes, my ears, and my lips.
May they always praise you.

Jesus, take pity on the souls
in purgatory who cannot receive
communion. Let them come
quickly to you.

Jesus, I love you. Help me
to love you more and more.

Here are two other well-known
prayers often said after communion.

PRAYER BEFORE A CRUCIFIX

Look down upon me,
good and gentle Jesus,
while before Your face
I humbly kneel and with burning
soul pray and beseech You
to fix deep in my heart
lively sentiments of faith,
hope and charity,
true contrition for my sins,
and a firm purpose of amendment.

While I contemplate,
with great love and tender pity,
Your five most precious wounds,
pondering over them within me
and calling to mind the words
which David, Your prophet,
said of You, my Jesus :

"They have pierced my hands
and my feet, they have injured
all my bones." Amen.

SOUL OF CHRIST

(This is a prayer of Saint Ignatius Loyola)

Soul of Christ, sanctify me.
Body of Christ, save me.
Blood of Christ, inebriate me.
Water from the side of Christ,
wash me.
Passion of Christ, strengthen me.
O good Jesus, hear me.
Within Your wounds, hide me.
Separated from you,
let me never be.
From the malignant enemy,
defend me.
At the hour of death, call me.
To come to You, bid me,
that I may praise You
in the company of Your saints,
for all eternity. Amen.

THE PLACE OF HOLY COMMUNION IN THE CHURCH

Holy Communion holds a central place in our Catholic religion for many reasons.

First of all, the bread and wine brought to the altar before the offering at Mass symbolizes us. We are making a gift of ourselves to God.

Second, this bread and wine is consecrated by the priest and is changed into the body and blood of Christ. Then it is offered to God as a continuation of Jesus' sacrifice for our redemption.

Third, the same transformed bread and wine is given to the congregation at Mass, so they are nourished by the very life of Christ. This is called Holy Communion.

Fourth, Holy Communion is also given to the sick and dying, to comfort and sometimes to heal them.

Fifth, the consecrated bread is kept in the tabernacle, so that whenever you go to visit a Catholic church, you know that Christ is truly present there.

WHEN TO RECEIVE
HOLY COMMUNION

The church encourages you to receive Holy Communion whenever you attend Mass.

You may always receive communion at Mass, unless you have committed a very serious sin. In this case, you will need to receive the Sacrament of Reconciliation first.

It is usually rare for a very young child to commit a serious sin.

If you are at Mass and you think you remember committing a serious sin, but are not absolutely sure, receive communion in the following way.

Before communion, tell Jesus in your heart you are sorry for that sin and for all the sins you may have committed.

Then go to communion.

Next time you receive the Sacrament of Reconciliation, mention your sin to the priest.

There is no need to worry about your sins. The important thing to remember is God loves you and Jesus wants to be with you.

That means they want you to receive Holy Communion whenever possible.

Chapter 8

RECONCILIATION

As a Catholic you have a special privilege in being able to celebrate the Sacrament of Reconciliation, whenever you may need to. At one time this sacrament was called "Penance" or "Confession".

It is easy to celebrate this sacrament.

And it is a beautiful sacrament, because if you have offended God, or others, or yourself, then things will need to be set right again. That's what reconciliation means—putting our hearts back together again in love. And that's something worth celebrating!

Reconciliation happens in the sacrament through God's forgiveness conveyed by the words of the priest.

In this sacrament, the priest takes the place of Jesus. You kneel or sit by him and tell him your sins. You tell him what things are not right with you. There is never any need to be afraid.

Then, as you would say it to Jesus, tell the priest you are sorry for the wrong you did.

And promise to try not doing anything that would separate you from God's love.

The priest may talk with you for a while. Be natural and comfortable with him. Listen to what he has to say. Do what he tells you to do.

Before you leave, he will bless you and give absolution. Those words bring the grace of forgiveness into your soul. The wounds in your soul begin to heal.

Forgiveness is something to celebrate. It means God never stops loving us. And Jesus helps sinners.

EXAMINING MY LIFE

Before meeting the priest for the Sacrament of Reconciliation, it is good to spend some time looking at your life. See what you have done since the last time you received Reconciliation.

Did you do things that were wrong?

Did you omit good things that your should have done?

Here are some questions you may ask yourself to help examine your life:

EXAMINATION

Do I think about God? Do I say thanks to Him every day for his many gifts? Do I ask Him to bless the people in my life?

Do I share with others the good things I have? My talents?

Do I ever help people who are poor, hungry or handicapped?

Do I treat fairly the boys and girls in my neighborhood and at school?

Do I speak about God with respect?

Do I respect my body and take good care of it?

Do I respect what belongs to other people?

Do I tell the truth always?

Am I willing to make up after a quarrel?

Am I willing to ask forgiveness when I hurt someone by my selfishness?

Do I really try to pray when I come to church, or do I spend time disturbing others?

Do I show my love to people who are sick or lonely?

JUST BEFORE THE SACRAMENT

Once you have examined your life and know the things you want to tell the priest, feel sorry for your sins with all your heart.

God will forgive any sin, no matter how serious, if only you are sorry and resolve not to do it again.

God knows we are weak and maybe will commit the same sins again. But he will forgive your same sins a thousand times as long as you are sorry.

Ask Jesus to help you to be sorry:

Jesus, I am sorry because I know that my sins and the sins of the world caused you to suffer and die on the cross.

Jesus, I am sorry because I know my sins can take me away from you, and I never want to be separated from you.

Jesus, I am sorry for my sins because you are so good and kind and forgiving. I do not want to hurt your Sacred Heart.

EASY STEPS
OF RECONCILIATION

When you are ready to confess your sins individually, here are some simple steps to follow:

First, when you go into the Reconciliation Room, say "Hello, Father," or greet him in some normal way.

Second, make the *Sign of the Cross* on your body. The priest will be blessing you at the same time.

Third, tell the priest what you have done wrong and, if necessary, why you did it. (Were you greedy, disobedient, selfish, spiteful, hurting others, or something else?)

Fourth, listen carefully to what the priest says to you. He will usually ask you to say a prayer or to do something to show you are sorry for your sins. He may ask you to say an *Act of Contrition*.

Fifth, listen as the priest says the

words of absolution and reconciliation. Remember, God is forgiving you. And you can be grateful for that.

Sixth, say "Thank you, Father," as you are leaving.

AFTER THE SACRAMENT

When you have left the priest, sit or kneel in the pews for a few minutes.

While you are there, be sure to say whatever the priest told you to say as a penance.

You may also say an *Act of Contrition*, if you did not say one while you were with the priest.

Here are two forms of an *Act of Contrition*.

Child's Act of Contrition

Lord God,
I trust in your goodness and mercy.

I am sorry
for all the wrong things I have done.
I am sorry
for all the good things
I have not done.
I want to love you with all my heart.

Act of Contrition

O my God,
I am heartily sorry
for having offended You,
and I detest all my sins,
because of Your just punishments,
but most of all
because they offend You, my God,
who are all good
and deserving of all love.
I firmly resolve,
with the help of Your grace,
to sin no more
and to avoid the near occasions
of sin. Amen

Chapter 9

MARY,
THE MOTHER OF JESUS

Catholics have a special love and devotion to Mary, the mother of Jesus; their favorite names for her are the Blessed Mother, the Blessed Virgin and Our Lady.

We pray to Mary as a privileged saint, one who gave human life to God's own son by being the mother of Jesus.

When we want to ask God for a special blessing or healing, we can ask the Blessed Mother to take our prayer and make it her own prayer to God.

Whenever Mary or one of the saints asks God for something on our behalf, we call it *intercession*. We say Mary is interceding for us.

Here are some prayers that will help you ask for Mary's intercession.

The Memorare

We believe God will never refuse any prayer of Mary. *The Memorare* expresses our confidence in the Blessed Mother as our intercessor.

Remember,
O most gracious Virgin Mary,
that never was it known
that anyone who fled
to your protection,
implored your help
or sought your intercession
was left unaided.
Inspired with this confidence,
I fly to you,
O Virgin of virgins, my Mother.
To you I come, before you I stand,
sinful and sorrowful.
O Mother of the Word Incarnate,
do not ignore my petitions,
but in your mercy
hear and answer me. Amen.

Hail, Holy Queen

Catholics often say this prayer after reciting the Rosary. But it is a beautiful prayer whenever you feel discouraged, sorrowful, or helpless.

Hail, holy Queen,
Mother of mercy!
Hail, our life,
our sweetness and hope!
To you do we cry,
poor banished children of Eve;
to you do we send up our sighs,
mourning and weeping
in this valley of tears!
Turn then, most gracious advocate,
your eyes of mercy toward us;
and after this, our exile,
show unto us the blessed
fruit of your womb, Jesus.
O clement, O loving,
O sweet Virgin Mary.

The Angelus

This prayer recalls the sacred moment when God announced to Mary that she would be mother of Jesus, who is the Word of God.

For centuries, when church bells rang at noontime and at six o'clock in the morning and evening, Christians would stop whatever they were doing and recite this prayer.

(If there are two people reciting the Angelus together, one says the V. lines, and the other says the R. lines. V stands for verse, R for response.)

V. *The angel of the Lord
declared unto Mary.*
R. *And she conceived
of the Holy Spirit.
Hail Mary, etc.*

V. *Behold the handmaid of the Lord.*

R. *Be it done unto me*
according to Thy word.
Hail Mary, etc.

V. *And the Word was made flesh.*
R. *And dwelt among us.*
Hail Mary, etc.

V. *Pray for us,*
O holy Mother of God.
R. *That we may be worthy*
of the promises of Christ.
Let us pray:

Pour forth, we beseech You,
O Lord, Your grace into our hearts,
that we, to whom
the Incarnation of Christ,
Your Son, was made known
by the message of an angel,
may, by His Passion and Cross,
be brought to the glory
of His Resurrection.
Through the same Christ our Lord.
Amen.

The Magnificat
(From Luke 1:46–55)

Mary herself prayed this prayer aloud, in front of her cousin Elizabeth, when she realized how blessed by God she was in being called to be the mother of Jesus.

*My soul proclaims
the greatness of the Lord,
and my spirit exults in God
my Savior, because He
has looked upon
His lowly handmaid.*

*Yes, from this day forward
all generations will call me blessed,
for the Almighty
has done great things for me,
holy is His Name;
and His mercy reaches
from age to age
for those who fear Him.*

*He has shown the power
of His arm, He has routed
the proud of heart.
He has pulled down princes
from their thrones
and exalted the lowly.
The hungry He has filled
with good things, while the rich
He has sent away empty.*

*He has come to the help
of Israel His servant,
mindful of His mercy—
according to the promise He made
to our ancestors—of his mercy
to Abraham and his descendants
forever.*

Chapter 10

SAINT JOSEPH

When you love Jesus and his mother Mary, you also love Joseph. The three of them together are called the Holy Family.

Joseph was close to Mary and Jesus. He watched over them, worked for them, and died in their arms.

His power is great with God. St. Teresa tells us that Joseph will never fail us. "Go to Saint Joseph," is her advice, whenever you need a favor, a grace, a help of any kind.

If you find it hard to be quiet, go to Joseph, for in all the New Testament not a single word of his is written down.

If you find it hard to be obedient, go to Joseph, for he was most obedient, even when he couldn't understand why.

If you find it hard to do your work, go to Joseph, for he was a hard worker and is the Patron Saint of workers.

Here are some prayers you might like to say to Saint Joseph:

Saint Joseph,
you loved the child Jesus
with all your heart.
Pray for me, a child
who needs your love.

Help me Joseph
in my earthly strife,
ever to lead a pure
and blameless life.

Saint Joseph,
please take care of me always,
now, and all through my life,
and especially
when I come to die.

I want to follow your example,
Saint Joseph, and love Jesus
and Mary as you did.
Good Saint Joseph pray for me.

You may also ask Saint Joseph to bless you. This is his blessing:

May the poverty of my little Jesus
be your riches; his sighs
and tears your consolation;
the love of his Infant Heart,
your treasure on earth;
and the sight of him,
your joy and reward in heaven.

Saint Joseph,
patron of those who die loving Jesus
and Mary, pray for us.

The Litany of Saint Joseph is on Page 142.

A HAPPY DEATH

St. Joseph is the Patron Saint of a happy death.

Many people are frightened of death and cannot imagine death being a happy experience.

But we who believe in Jesus know that Jesus has passed through death to eternal life, and we know that if we love him he will lead us through death to a new life.

For a Christian, death is not the end of life, but the beginning of a new existence. Jesus told us many times that life on the other side of death is beautiful for those who love God.

Saint Joseph, who died happily in the arms of Jesus and Mary, knew this. So we pray to him to make our death a happy one, too.

Saint Joseph, patron of the dying, pray my death will be a happy one.

Chapter 11

A CHILD'S
ALBUM OF SAINTS

In his letters, Saint Paul referred to early Christians as Saints. According to him, everyone who believed in Jesus was a Saint. So Paul would have called you a child Saint.

Through the centuries, the church has called Saints only those holy people who were canonized after their death. These Saints lived holy lives and usually performed miracles.

Catholics pray to Saints for special help and assistance. Saints are like good friends. They already live in heaven, but they also know what it is like to live on earth.

Saints sometimes help us directly, as

good friends do. Or they can pray to God for us. Or they can join their prayers with ours to God.

There are two important things to remember about Saints.

First, they are already with God.

Second, they are most willing and eager to help you.

God is good, and will hear their prayers for you.

Here are some of the Saints you will want to know.

Saint Anne

Saint Anne is Mary's mother. She is called Good Saint Anne because when you pray to her, she never fails to help. The Blessed Virgin Mary was her little girl.

Dear Saint Anne,
I come to you as a little child.
Please whisper my name

to your own child,
the Blessed Virgin Mary.
I hope one day to be with you
in heaven and to see Jesus
and Mary there.

Saint Anthony

Saint Anthony is most known for helping find things that get lost. All through life, you will lose things. Whether it's something big or very little, ask Saint Anthony. And if he helps you find what you lost, be sure to say aloud, "Thank you, Saint Anthony!"

Dear Saint Anthony,
pray for me to Little Jesus,
whom you held lovingly
in your arms.
Obtain for me the grace to love him
with all my heart.

Saint Francis of Assisi

Saint Francis was known for his love of nature. He was able to talk to birds, fish and other animals.

Dear Saint Francis
teach me to know
all the lovely creatures
that live in our world.
When I am tempted to be harsh,
help me to be gentle and kind.

Saint Elizabeth Ann Seton

Saint Elizabeth Ann is also known as Mother Seton. She was the first American-born to be canonized a Saint. She was a hard-working woman who managed to do many things for God. She founded schools to teach children.

Dear Mother Seton,
you are very special to us Americans

and you are very special to children.
Help me learn about God,
and fill me with love for the church.

Saint Clare

Saint Clare, a wealthy and beautiful young girl, left her home in Assisi to follow a life of simplicity. She was a good friend of Saint Francis. She knew how to pray and will help you when you find it hard to pray.

Dear Saint Clare,
help me to realize
that loving God
is more important
than having a lot of money
and rich possessions.
Help me to gather
a fortune of divine grace
so that I can be with you in heaven.

Saint Bernadette

Saint Bernadette was a little French girl, to whom Mary, the mother of Jesus, appeared at Lourdes. Mary told Bernadette "I am the Immaculate Conception." In the waters at Lourdes, where the vision happened, many miraculous cures have occurred.

Dear Saint Bernadette,
remember when
you were a young person
like I am?

Please tell Mary
that I am your friend.

I will come to you
and ask for special favors
when I need them.

Fill my life with grace.
I want to see Mary, too.

Saint Martin De Porres

Saint Martin lived his life in Peru caring for the slaves who were brought to Peru from Africa. He had a special love for the sick and performed many miracles in his lifetime. He is the Patron of Social Justice.

Dear Saint Martin,
please pray for all those who suffer
because of prejudice
and discrimination.
When I think I am more important
to God than somebody else,
remind me of your love
for the African slaves.

Saint Joan of Arc

Saint Joan was a very brave young French woman. She often heard voices coming from God. They told her to lead her people to freedom. Her love for God was strong and pure.

Dear Saint Joan,
help me to be strong and pure
in my love of God. Help me
to listen closely to the words of God
and the ways he will touch my life.
Help me to be brave
in following God's call.

Saint Aloysius

Saint Aloysius, even though he came from a rich family, chose to spend his life caring for the sick and teaching street children about the love of God. He is the patron of young people, and a model of innocence.

Dear Saint Aloysius,
Patron of Youth, protect me
from the dangers of life
that can corrupt me. Pray for me
that I may be a good child
and eventually be with you
in heaven.

Saint John Bosco

Saint John dedicated his life to caring for the abandoned boys who roamed uncared for on the streets of the industrial cities. Today, his followers care for needy children in all continents of the world.

Dear Saint John,
you were always on the lookout
for forgotten children.
Sometimes I feel abandoned, too.
Help me to realize
that I have friends like you
in heaven, and I will
never be lonely.

Saint Maria Goretti

Saint Maria, a gentle young girl, was abused and beaten by a man. Dying in the hospital, she forgave the man who attacked her. Many miracles are attributed to her.

Dear Saint Maria,
I often do not know
how to respond to the wickedness
I see. Help me to be like you.
Help me to forgive those
who do me harm.

Saint Therese of the Child Jesus

Saint Therese, also called the Little Flower, spent her life hidden in prayer. She dedicated her life to saving souls. Without ever leaving her convent, she became a missionary all over the world by the power of her prayers.

Dear Saint Therese,
help me to pray
fervently to God.
I want to remember to pray
for so many different people
and sometimes I forget.
Be my friend and lead me to God
and together we shall pray to Jesus
and Mary.

Chapter 12

THE WAY OF THE CROSS

This is the story of Jesus' sorrowful journey to his death on Good Friday. The Way of the Cross has 14 stations or stopping places. These are moments that help us understand the deep love Jesus has for us.

Every Catholic church has the stations of the cross on its walls. People often make the stations in church, especially during Lent. Use this book to help you as you go from station to station.

You may begin by kneeling before the main altar and telling Jesus that you wish to gain all the graces you can for yourself, your friends and relatives. Tell Jesus you also wish graces for the souls in purgatory who are waiting for us to pray for them so they soon can go to God.

At each station, picture in your imagination what is happening to Jesus, then tell him how you feel and how much you love him.

It may make you feel sad and sorrowful to imagine the suffering and pain Jesus felt on the way to his death. But remember he did it for you and me, so that we could have all our sins forgiven and live forever with God and all the Saints in heaven. And for this we should thank Jesus again and again.

We begin each station by saying the prayer:

We adore you, O Christ, and bless you,

Because by your Holy Cross you have redeemed the world!

FIRST STATION

Jesus is Condemned to Death

Picture Jesus standing before Pilate, the judge. He is innocent of every crime, but the judge condemns him. And he begins the journey to his death, the way of the cross.

Tell Jesus you know that it is really the evil thoughts, words and actions of people that condemn him. Tell him you are sorry for all your sins and the sins of others.

Our Father, Hail Mary, Glory be, etc.

SECOND STATION

Jesus Takes the Cross Upon His shoulders

Picture Jesus with his shoulders all bruised and bleeding from the soldiers' whips. What pain the heavy cross gives him when they place it on him.

Tell Jesus you know how much it must hurt, and how gladly you would help him carry the cross if you could.

Our Father, Hail Mary, Glory be, etc.

THIRD STATION

Jesus Falls the First Time

Picture Jesus weak and tired from all the cruel punishment he has received. The blood from the crown of thorns is rolling down his face. The cross is so heavy he falls to the ground.

Tell Jesus that you love him and that you know how it hurts when he falls. Tell him you are his friend.

Our Father, Hail Mary, Glory be, etc.

FOURTH STATION

Jesus Meets His Mother

Picture Jesus turning the corner on the road to Calvary and seeing his mother. He wishes she did not have to see him like this, but her eyes tell him that she loves him and that her heart aches for him.

Tell Jesus that your heart aches for him, too. Promise that you always will love his mother and will pray to her often.

Our Father, Hail Mary, Glory be, etc.

FIFTH STATION

*Simon of Cyrene
Helps Jesus Carry the Cross*

Picture a stranger, Simon. The soldiers pull him out of the crowd to help Jesus carry his cross. Without help, Jesus might have died on the way. The eyes of Jesus give Simon a grateful look and a promise of eternal life.

Tell Jesus you are happy that Simon was chosen to share his heavy cross. Tell him how you will be grateful to those who help you, and ask Jesus to bless them.

Our Father, Hail Mary, Glory be, etc.

SIXTH STATION

Veronica Wipes the Face of Jesus

Picture the beautiful face of Jesus all covered with sweat, dust and blood. A good lady, touched by his suffering, runs to him and wipes his face clean with her veil.

Tell Jesus how you long to see his face and touch it. Ask him to let your heart be like Veronica's heart, filled with tender love and pity for him.

Our Father, Hail Mary, Glory be, etc.

SEVENTH STATION

Jesus Falls a Second Time

Picture the heavy cross again forcing the exhausted Jesus to his knees. See the cruel soldiers, wanting only to get a job done, kick and push Jesus to get him moving again.

Tell Jesus how good he is to suffer for the sins of the world. Ask him to make you as patient and courageous as he is. Say to him, "I love you".

Our Father, Hail Mary, Glory be, etc.

EIGHTH STATION

Jesus Speaks to Women from Jerusalem

Picture Jesus meeting some women from Jerusalem who are sobbing to see him being led away to death. Hear Jesus tell the women to weep not for him but for sinners who refuse God's forgiveness.

Tell Jesus you know how willing he is to be of help to others. Let him know that you will always come to him for forgiveness whenever you sin.

Our Father, Hail Mary, Glory be, etc.

NINTH STATION

Jesus Falls a Third Time

Picture Jesus near Calvary Hill and

thinking of all the pain he has yet to suffer. His strength leaves him, he staggers and falls to the ground.

Tell Jesus you know how hard it is to have courage when you are scared, how hard it is to be in pain and not know what to do. Comfort Jesus who loves you.

Our Father, Hail Mary, Glory be, etc.

TENTH STATION

Jesus is Stripped of His Garments

Picture Jesus on top of the hill. The angry crowd is standing around staring at him. See the guards pull off his clothes, opening again the wounds that had dried and stuck to his garments.

Tell Jesus, who is wounded and bleeding for all of us, that you love him.

Tell him you want to be a kind and loving person, to make up for all the thoughtless cruelty of people.

Our Father, Hail Mary, Glory be, etc.

ELEVENTH STATION

Jesus is Nailed to the Cross

Picture Jesus lying on the wood of the cross, his arms and feet stretched out. See and hear the soldiers hammer nails through his hands and feet.

Tell Jesus you are sorry for his pain, but are thankful for his love. Tell him you love his feet that walked to people in need, and you love his hands that gently healed the sick.

Our Father, Hail Mary, Glory be, etc.

TWELFTH STATION

Jesus Dies on the Cross

Picture Jesus patiently hanging on the cross for three long hours. He speaks kindly to the good thief, forgives his enemies, and consoles his mother and his friends who are nearby.

Tell Jesus how you would like to have him speak lovingly to you. Ask him to pour his love on you, and tell him you want to return his love.

Our Father, Hail Mary, Glory be, etc.

THIRTEENTH STATION

Jesus is Taken Down from the Cross

Picture Jesus' friends gently and reverently taking his dead body down from the cross. See them remove the nails from his hands and feet, and put his body in the arms of his mother.

Tell Mary how you would like to have been at her side at that sorrowful moment to comfort her. Tell her how much you love her son Jesus.

Our Father, Hail Mary, Glory be, etc.

FOURTEENTH STATION

Jesus is Laid in the Tomb

Picture the men and women carefully wrapping Jesus in burial cloth and placing his body in the tomb. See the sad faces on Jesus' friends as they seal the tomb with a large rock and begin walking back to the city.

Tell Jesus you are sad for his friends,

but you know he has descended among the dead to set them free. Tell Jesus you know he will rise again and ask him to let you live with him forever.

Our Father, Hail Mary, Glory be, etc.

Chapter 13

THE ROSARY

The Rosary is a very special way of praying. Rosary beads help you pray the Rosary.

It is easy to learn to pray the Rosary because you know all the prayers by heart: *The Apostles' Creed, Our Father, Hail Mary, and Glory Be.* The best way to learn is for someone to show you how to use the Rosary beads.

After you know how, you may ask your parents or guardians to get you your very own Rosary beads.

You may take them to a priest and have them blessed especially for you.

The Rosary is a prayer that pleases Our Lady. When you say it, you will be showing her that you love her and wish to be her special child.

Here is the special part of the Rosary prayer. While you are saying the words of the Hail Mary, you let your imagination think about a certain story in the lives of Jesus and Mary.

There are three sets of stories or mysteries: Five Joyful ones, five Sorrowful ones and five Glorious ones.

THE JOYFUL MYSTERIES

The Five Joyful Mysteries are used on Mondays and Thursdays. As you pray the Rosary, picture in your mind each of the following five stories one by one.

1. The Annunciation

Picture the Angel Gabriel appearing to the Blessed Virgin Mary telling her she is to be the mother of God. Think of Mary saying "yes" to God's invitation. Picture the Holy Spirit conceiving the baby who will be Jesus, the Son of God.

2. The Visitation

See Mary happily walking to her cousin Elizabeth's house to tell her the good news about the baby Jesus inside her. Hear the two women sharing their joy, for each will soon be mothers.

3. The Nativity

See Mary and Joseph in the stable with the shepherds and animals. See the infant Jesus lying in a manger of straw. The Son of God has been born.

4. The Presentation

Picture Mary and Joseph in the big temple presenting their child Jesus to God. The Holy Man, Simeon, holds Jesus in his arms and gives thanks to God that the Savior of the world has come.

5. *The Finding in the Temple*

Picture Mary and Joseph searching for the child Jesus all through Jerusalem. They thought he was lost. See how relieved they are to find him safe in the temple.

THE SORROWFUL MYSTERIES

The Five Sorrowful Mysteries are used on Tuesdays and Fridays. As you pray this set of mysteries, picture in your mind each of the following five sorrowful stories one by one.

1. *The Agony in the Garden*

Picture Jesus praying in the Garden of Olives, afraid of the suffering he knows will soon come to him. He is in such agony that drops of blood and sweat break through his skin and trickle to the ground. See him find the strength to bear his Passion, to redeem the human race.

2. *The Scourging at the Pillar*

Picture Jesus, now in the hands of cruel soldiers, who have been given permission to whip him. See Jesus tied to a pillar and cruelly beaten. Think how his body is bloody and racked with pain.

3. *The Crowning With Thorns*

Picture Jesus surrounded by soldiers who mock him, laugh and spit at him. See them weave some thorn bushes into a king's crown and press it into his head.

4. *The Carrying of the Cross*

Picture Jesus being shoved and pushed like an animal. See him carrying the heavy cross, exhausted, slowly staggering along the road to the hill where he is to be crucified.

5. The Crucifixion

Picture Jesus nailed to the cross, hanging for three hours. Life drains out of him and angry crowds torment him. Hear him say that he undergoes his Passion for love of us. Always remember, he dies loving us.

THE GLORIOUS MYSTERIES

The Five Glorious Mysteries are used on Wednesdays, Saturdays and Sundays. As you pray this set of mysteries, picture in your mind each of the following five happy stories one by one.

1. The Resurrection

Picture how Jesus conquers death and on Easter Sunday morning emerges from the tomb. See him visiting his mother and comforting his frightened friends. Hear him assuring them he will never die again.

2. *The Ascension*

Picture Jesus, forty days after Easter, among his disciples, giving them his final instructions. See him being lifted out of their sight, and being carried into the presence of God his Father in heaven. Be happy for Jesus who has finished his mission on earth.

3. *The Descent of the Holy Spirit*

Picture the timid disciples together in their meeting room early in the morning. Hear a mighty wind blow, and see tongues of fire burning above each of them. Feel how they are filled with strength by the Holy Spirit.

4. *The Assumption of Mary*

Picture Mary, the mother of Jesus, as she lies on her bed, dying. Imagine how the angels of God carry her beautiful body into heaven so she can be with her son Jesus once more and live with him forever and ever.

5. *The Crowning of Mary*

Picture the special moment in heaven when Mary arrives. Imagine the great celebration in her honor as the Blessed Mother is crowned Queen of Heaven by Jesus, her Son.

Chapter 14

SEVEN SACRAMENTS

Sacraments are outward visible signs of God's inward grace given at special moments in a person's life.

Christ instituted seven sacraments. They are used to help build and maintain the life of the people of God.

Some sacraments—baptism, confirmation, marriage and holy orders—are received only once. The others—reconciliation, communion, and anointing—may be received more than once.

BAPTISM

The first sacrament we receive is baptism. It makes us members of the church, part of the Body of Christ. Baptism is called christening.

It is performed by pouring water on a person's forehead and at the same time saying the words, "I baptize you in the name of the Father, and of the Son, and of the Holy Spirit. Amen."

When people are baptized as infants, baptism becomes a naming ceremony as well. While baptism is usually performed by a priest, in an emergency any believer in Jesus may baptize.

CONFIRMATION

This second sacrament is also part of a person's introduction into the church. Confirmation bestows the special seal or mark of the Holy Spirit.

While baptism makes you a member of the church, Confirmation gives you the special spiritual energy to make Jesus known in the world. It also gives you the courage to live the way Jesus would like you to live.

Confirmation is usually administered only by a bishop; sometimes by a specially designated priest.

HOLY EUCHARIST

Being baptized gives you the right to receive Holy Communion, the food of Christians. The church does not give communion to children too young to understand that the bread is the body of Christ.

Young people are prepared in Christian Doctrine classes and at home to receive first Holy Communion.

Communion is often called the greatest sacrament because Christ himself is present in the consecrated bread and wine.

The eucharistic bread is transformed into Christ by the priest during mass. The transformed bread is offered to God as a sacrifice and then given to the people of God as spiritual food.

In churches, consecrated bread is kept in the tabernacle. So, when people visit a church, they know that Christ is present in a special way. A vigil light is kept burning there at all times to tell people that Christ is present.

(See Chapter 7 on Holy Communion.)

RECONCILIATION

This sacrament brings us God's forgiveness through a priest. All we need do is to confess our sins sincerely, have sorrow for them and a firm intention of avoiding sin in the future. This sacrament used to be called "Penance" or "Confession."

The grace of this sacrament gives us the help of Jesus to overcome habits of sin and it makes us holy and one with the people of God. It reconciles us with God and the church.

(See Chapter 8 on Celebrating the Sacrament of Reconciliation.)

ANOINTING OF THE SICK

This is the sacrament for those who are seriously ill, the infirm and the very old. It used to be given only to those who were in very serious danger of death. At that time it was called "Last Rites," "Extreme Unction," or "Viaticum," which meant help for the journey into death.

Today, the sacrament of the sick sanctifies sufferings, increases grace, forgives sins and makes us ready for heaven.

The Anointing sometimes cures an illness and may heal the body as well as the soul.

This sacrament is administered by priests and deacons.

HOLY ORDERS

This sacrament gives the special power of Jesus to priests. This includes the power to forgive sins in Jesus' name, the power to anoint the sick, the power to change bread and wine into the body and blood of Christ, and the power to perpetuate Jesus' sacrifice, which is the Mass.

Through Holy Orders, priests and bishops receive the Spirit's grace to guide the church and take care of the people of God.

MATRIMONY

This sacrament is received when a husband and wife pronounce their marriage vows. It gives the grace for two people to join their lives together until death.

People often think it is the priest who performs this sacrament, but it is really the husband and wife who perform it for each other. The priest is only the official church witness of this sacrament.

This sacrament also gives people the grace to be good mothers and fathers to their children.

Usually, when someone receives a sacrament for the first time, a card or certificate is given. You will want to save these important documents.

The priest also keeps a record of the sacraments you receive in the Church Records.

For example, if you need to prove you were baptized and cannot find your baptismal certificate, you may ask the priest to look in the records of the church where you received this sacrament.

Chapter 15

GUIDES
FOR CHRISTIAN LIVING

Many rules, laws and commandments are given to us by God and the church to help us live our lives as good Christians.

For Christians, the most important commandment, above all others, is love.

In the early church, people used to say about Christians, "See how they love one another!"

Jesus told us to love each other as he loved us. If we keep his commandment of love, all the others will be easy.

The Ten Commandments
(From Exodus 20:1–17)

The Ten Commandments come to us from the Old Testament, the earliest part of the Bible. They were written on tablets of stone which Moses brought from the mountain where he met God in prayer.

1. I am the Lord your God. You shall not have strange gods before Me.

2. You shall not take the Name of the Lord your God in vain.

3. Remember to keep holy the Lord's Day.

4. Honor your father and your mother.

5. You shall not kill.

6. You shall not commit adultery.

7. You shall not steal.

8. You shall not bear false witness against your neighbor.

9. You shall not covet your neighbor's wife.

10. You shall not covet your neighbor's goods.

Jesus' Commandment of Love
(From Matthew 22:37–40)

When the teachers in Israel asked Jesus which of the commandments was the most important, he answered this way:

"You must love the Lord your God with all your heart, with all your soul, and with all your mind. This is the greatest and the first commandment. The second resembles it: You must love your neighbor as yourself. On these two commandments depend the whole law, and the prophets also."

The Six Precepts of the Church

The church has six precepts which are the major duties of Catholics. These precepts help us show our unity with the people of God.

1. To keep holy the day of the Lord's Resurrection. (This means to worship God by participating in Mass every Sunday and holy day of obligation.)

2. To fast and abstain on the appointed days. (This precept is obligatory only for adults; it shows how Christians put the love of God above all things.)

3. To celebrate the Sacrament of Reconciliation at least once a year. (Annual confession is obligatory only if serious sin is involved.)

4. To receive Holy Communion at least once a year during Lent or the Easter season. (Of course you will want to receive the Eucharist much more often.)

5. To strengthen and support the church. (This includes helping your parish priest, your parish community, the Holy Father and the people of God all over the world.)

6. To observe the marriage laws of the church. (Although this precept does not apply directly to you, it reminds your parents and guardians to train you in the Christian faith by their example and word.)

The Eight Beatitudes
(From Matthew 5:3-10)

Jesus spoke about eight kinds of people we normally feel sorry for because they are not rich, powerful and very honored. But God loves them so much they are blessed. Here are eight kinds of people God loves with a special love.

- Blessed are they who hunger and thirst
  for holiness:
  they shall have their fill.

- Blessed are they who show mercy:
  mercy shall be theirs.

- Blessed are the single-hearted:
  they shall see God.

- Blessed are the peacemakers:
  they shall be called sons of God.

- Blessed are those persecuted for
  holiness' sake:
  the reign of God is theirs.

- Blessed are the poor in spirit:
  the reign of God is theirs.

- Blessed are the sorrowing:
  they shall be consoled.

- Blessed are the lowly:
  they shall inherit the land.

The Chief Corporal Works of Mercy
(From Matthew 25:35-40)

Jesus asks us to take care of people who are physically suffering and in need. We are to look upon them as if they were Jesus, himself. Jesus said, "As long as you did it for one of these, the least of my brothers or sisters, you did it to me." The word *Corporal* refers to kindnesses we do for people that have to do with their *bodies*.

- To feed the hungry.
- To give drink to the thirsty.
- To clothe the naked.
- To visit the imprisoned.
- To shelter the homeless.
- To visit the sick.
- To bury the dead.

Jesus said, "I assure you, anyone who gives you a drink of water because you belong to Christ will not go without a reward" (Mark 9:41).

The Chief Spiritual Works of Mercy

Mercy means being kind in a caring way. Spiritual refers to the kindnesses we do for people's minds, hearts and spirits.

- To admonish the sinner.
- To instruct the ignorant.
- To counsel the doubtful.
- To comfort the sorrowful.
- To bear wrongs patiently.
- To forgive all injuries.
- To pray for the living and the dead.

Chapter 16

THE LITANIES

Litanies are a favorite way of praying by Catholics as a group. A leader is appointed to read the litany of names or invocations, usually addressed to Our Lord, Our Lady or other Saints. After each name, all the others respond with a petition, such as "Pray for us" or "Have mercy on us."

Here are some of the most popular litanies.

Litany of the Sacred Heart

This is a litany that names many wonderful ways to speak of the love that lives in Jesus' heart.

Lord, have mercy
Christ, have mercy
Lord, have mercy.

Christ, hear us.
Christ, graciously hear us.
God the Father of heaven,* have mercy on us,
  (repeat)
God the Son, Redeemer of the world,*
God the Holy Spirit,
Holy Trinity, one God,
Heart of Jesus, Son of the eternal Father,
Heart of Jesus, formed by the Holy Spirit
  in the womb of the Virgin Mother,
Heart of Jesus,
  substantially united to the Word of God,
Heart of Jesus, of infinite majesty,
Heart of Jesus, sacred temple of God,
Heart of Jesus, tabernacle of the Most High,
Heart of Jesus,
  house of God and gate of heaven,
Heart of Jesus, burning furnace of charity,
Heart of Jesus, abode of justice and love,
Heart of Jesus, full of goodness and love,
Heart of Jesus, abyss of all virtues,
Heart of Jesus, most worthy of all praise,
Heart of Jesus, king and center of all praise,
Heart of Jesus, king and center of all hearts,
Heart of Jesus, in whom are all the treasures
  of wisdom and knowledge,
Heart of Jesus,
  in whom dwells the fullness of divinity,
Heart of Jesus,
  in whom the Father is well pleased,

133

Heart of Jesus,
   of whose fullness we have all received,
Heart of Jesus, desire of the everlasting hills,
Heart of Jesus, patient and most merciful,
Heart of Jesus, enriching all who invoke You,
Heart of Jesus, fountain of life and holiness,
Heart of Jesus, propitiation for our sins,
Heart of Jesus, loaded down with opprobrium,
Heart of Jesus, bruised for our offenses,
Heart of Jesus, obedient unto death,
Heart of Jesus, pierced with a lance,
Heart of Jesus, source of all consolation,
Heart of Jesus, our life and resurrection,
Heart of Jesus, our peace and reconciliation,
Heart of Jesus, victim for our sins,
Heart of Jesus,
   salvation of those who trust in You,
Heart of Jesus, hope of those who die in You,
Heart of Jesus, delight of all the saints,

Lamb of God,
who take away the sins of the world,
   spare us, O Lord.
Lamb of God,
who take away the sins of the world,
   graciously hear us, O Lord.
Lamb of God,
who take away the sins of the world,
   have mercy on us.
Jesus, meek and humble of heart.
   Make our hearts like Yours.

Let us Pray:
Almighty and eternal God,
look upon the heart
of Your most beloved Son
and upon the praises
and satisfaction which He
offers You in the name of sinners;
and to those who implore Your mercy,
in Your great goodness,
grant them forgiveness
in the Name of the same Jesus Christ,
Your Son, who lives
and reigns with You forever
and ever. Amen.

Litany of the Holy Name of Jesus

Christians love the name of Jesus and say it often in a prayerful way. You may recite this litany to make up for all the times people use Jesus' beautiful name thoughtlessly or wickedly.

Lord, have mercy on us
Christ, have mercy on us.
Lord, have mercy on us.

Jesus, hear us.
Jesus, graciously hear us.
God the Father of heaven,
have mercy on us.

God the Son,
Redeemer of the world,* have mercy on us,
  (repeat)
God the Holy Ghost,*
Holy Trinity, one God,

Jesus, Son of the Living God,
Jesus, Splendor of the Father,
Jesus, Brightness of Eternal Light,
Jesus, King of glory,
Jesus, Sun of Justice,
Jesus, Son of the Virgin Mary,
Jesus, amiable,
Jesus, admirable,
Jesus, the powerful God,
Jesus, Father of the world to come,
Jesus, Angel of the great Council,
Jesus, most powerful,
Jesus, most patient,
Jesus, most obedient,
Jesus, meek and humble of heart,
Jesus, Lover of Chastity,
Jesus, Lover of us,
Jesus, God of Peace,
Jesus, Author of Life,
Jesus, Model of Virtues,
Jesus, zealous for souls,
Jesus, our God,
Jesus, our Refuge,
Jesus, Father of the Poor,
Jesus, Treasure of the Faithful,
Jesus, good Shepherd,

Jesus, true Light,
Jesus, eternal Wisdom,
Jesus, infinite Goodness,
Jesus, our Way and our Life,
Jesus, Joy of Angels,
Jesus, King of the Patriarchs,
Jesus, Master of the Apostles,
Jesus, Teacher of the Evangelists,
Jesus, Strength of Martyrs,
Jesus, Light of Confessors,
Jesus, Purity of Virgins,
Jesus, Crown of all Saints,

Be merciful, spare us, O Jesus!
Be merciful, hear us, O Jesus!

From all evil,** deliver us, O Jesus!
  (repeat)
From all sin,**
From your wrath,
From the snares of the devil,
From the spirit of fornication,
From eternal death,
From the neglect of Your inspirations
By the mystery of Your holy incarnation,
By Your nativity,
By Your infancy,
By Your most divine life.
By Your labors,
By Your agony and passion,
By Your cross and dereliction,
By Your languors,

By Your death and burial
By Your resurrection,
By Your ascension,
By Your institution of the Most
    Blessed Sacrament,
By Your joys,
By Your glory,

Lamb of God,
Who takes away the sins of the world,
    spare us, O Jesus.
Lamb of God,
Who takes away the sins of the world,
    hear us, O Jesus!
Lamb of God,
Who takes away the sins of the world,
    have mercy on us, O Jesus!
Jesus, hear us.
Jesus, graciously hear us.

Let us Pray.
O Lord Jesus Christ, Who said:
"Ask, and you shall receive;
seek, and you shall find,
knock, and it shall be opened to you;"
mercifullly attend to our supplications, and
grant us the gift of Your Divine Charity that
we may ever love You with our whole hearts
and never desist from praising You.

Give us, O Lord, a perpetual fear and love
of Your holy Name, for You never cease

to direct and govern by Your grace
those whom You instruct
in the solidity of Your Love;
Who lives and reigns world without end.
Amen.

Litany of the Blessed Virgin Mary
(Litany of Loreto)

This litany enables us to speak aloud the many lovely names that have been given to Our Lady.

Lord, have mercy.
Christ, have mercy.
Lord, have mercy.

Christ, hear us.
Christ, graciously hear us.

God, the Father of heaven, have mercy on us.
God the Son, Redeemer of the world,
   have mercy on us.
God the Holy Spirit, have mercy on us.
Holy Trinity, one God, have mercy on us.
Holy Mary, pray for us.
Holy Mother of God, pray for us.
Holy Virgin of virgins, pray for us.
Mother of Christ, pray for us.
Mother of divine grace, pray for us.
Mother most pure, pray for us.

Mother most chaste, pray for us.
Mother inviolate, pray for us.
Mother undefiled, pray for us.
Mother most amiable, pray for us.
Mother most admirable, pray for us.
Mother of good counsel, pray for us.
Mother of our Creator, pray for us.
Mother of our Savior, pray for us.
Virgin most prudent, pray for us.
Virgin most venerable, pray for us.
Virgin most renowned, pray for us
Virgin most powerful, pray for us.
Virgin most merciful, pray for us.
Virgin most faithful, pray for us.
Mirror of justice, pray for us.
Seat of wisdom, pray for us.
Cause of our joy, pray for us.
Spiritual vessel, pray for us.
Vessel of honor, pray for us.
Singular vessel of devotion, pray for us.
Mystical rose, pray for us.
Tower of David, pray for us.
Tower of ivory, pray for us.
House of gold, pray for us.
Ark of the covenant, pray for us.
Gate of heaven, pray for us.
Morning Star, pray for us.
Health of the sick, pray for us.
Refuge of sinners, pray for us.
Comforter of the afflicted, pray for us.
Help of Christians, pray for us.

Queen of angels, *pray for us.*
Queen of patriarchs, *pray for us.*
Queen of prophets, *pray for us.*
Queen of Apostles, *pray for us.*
Queen of martyrs, *pray for us.*
Queen of confessors, *pray for us.*
Queen of virgins, *pray for us.*
Queen of all saints, *pray for us.*
Queen conceived without original sin,
Queen assumed into heaven, *pray for us*
Queen of the most holy Rosary, *pray for us.*
Queen of peace, *pray for us.*

Lamb of God,
  who take away the sins of the world,
    graciously hear us, O Lord.
Lamb of God,
  who take away the sins of the world,
    have mercy on us.
Pray for us, O holy Mother of God
That we may be made worthy
  of the promises of Christ.

Let us pray:

Grant, we beg you, O Lord God,
that we Your servants
may enjoy lasting health of mind and body,
and by the glorious intercession
of the Blessed Mary, ever Virgin,
be delivered from present sorrow
and enter into the joy of eternal happiness.
Through Christ our Lord. Amen.

Litany of Saint Joseph

This litany describes the many virtues of Saint Joseph. Because Saint Joseph lived and died in the presence of Jesus and Mary, you can pray to Saint Joseph so that you too will be able to live and die happily in the presence of Jesus, Mary and Joseph.

Lord, have mercy on us.
Christ, have mercy on us.
Lord, have mercy on us.

Christ, hear us.
Christ, graciously hear us.

God the Father of Heaven,
have mercy on us.

Joseph most faithful,* pray for us,
   (repeat)
Mirror of patience,*
Lover of poverty,
Model of laborers,
Ornament of domestic life,
Protector of virgins,
Pillar of families,
Consolation of the afflicted,
Hope of the sick,
Patron of the dying,

Terror of the demons,
Protector of the Holy Church,
Lamb of God,
Who takes away the sins of the world,
spare us, O Lord!
Lamb of God,
Who takes away the sins of the world,
graciously hear us, O Lord!
Lamb of God,
Who takes away the sins of the world,
have mercy on us, O Lord!
He made him master of His house.
And ruler of all his possessions.

Let us Pray.
O God, who deigned to elect Blessed Joseph
spouse of Your most holy Mother;
grant, we beseech You, that we may have him,
whom we venerate as our protector on earth,
as our intercessor in heaven.
Who lives and reigns world without end.
Amen.

PRINTED IN BELGIUM BY

proost
INTERNATIONAL BOOK PRODUCTION